IMAGES
of America

JEWS OF OAKLAND
AND BERKELEY

IMAGES
of America

JEWS OF OAKLAND AND BERKELEY

Frederick Isaac

ARCADIA
PUBLISHING

Published by Arcadia Publishing
Charleston SC, Chicago IL, Portsmouth NH, San Francisco CA

Printed in the United States of America

Library of Congress Control Number: 2009920005

For all general information contact Arcadia Publishing at:
Telephone 843-853-2070
Fax 843-853-0044
E-mail sales@arcadiapublishing.com
For customer service and orders:
Toll-Free 1-888-313-2665

Visit us on the Internet at www.arcadiapublishing.com

CONTENTS

ACKNOWLEDGMENTS

Responsibility for an enterprise such as this must be spread far and wide. The collection of items about the history of a community represents the breadth of its interests. This book is no different. My thanks go first to the Magnes Museum in Berkeley. James Leventhal invited me to undertake this project; Lara Michaels, the archivist in the Western Jewish History Center, was invaluable in collecting and reviewing material with me; and Francesco Spagnolo, the head curator, was involved and interested in every stage of the process. My appreciation to those who spoke to me is enormous; they gave time, insights, and a range of perspectives that allowed me to expand my scope. The many people throughout the community who provided images are the true heroes of this project. Without them, there is no history of the Jews of the East Bay. I am enormously grateful for their confidence in me and their interest in the subject. Many of them are named in the credits. Within the text, please note that "federation" refers to the current Jewish Community Federation of the Greater East Bay. Special thanks must be given to Fred Rosenbaum, the true historian of the Jews of the Bay Area. His 1976 history of the East Bay, *Free to Choose: The making of a Jewish Community in the American West*, was the source of many of the ideas in this book. My editor at Arcadia, Kelly Reed, has been quietly insistent and endlessly patient with this process and the author's issues. Finally, my wife Robin has listened to all the stories and suggested her own ideas.

INTRODUCTION

One of Gertrude Stein's most famous statements concerned her childhood hometown of Oakland. "There is no *there* there," she said in *Everybody's Autobiography*, and the quip has stuck for over half a century. Like many such aphorisms, it has a grain of truth. Oakland has felt neglected for its entire history in favor of San Francisco, its grand neighbor across the bay. In fact, Oakland has a solid history and achievements that would have been enough for most cities. Its fate, however, has put it in the shadows, and its value has been overlooked.

The Jewish history of Oakland goes back to the early 1860s. While there had been a few Jewish settlers during the Gold Rush era, their first significant communal effort took place in 1865, when they purchased land from the Mountain View Cemetery Association and created a Jewish burial ground they called Home of Eternity. As the city grew, more Jews found their way west; the first synagogue, First Hebrew Congregation, was founded in the mid-1870s.

Over the next 40 years, the community grew and prospered, and Jewish businesses and organizations developed alongside them. Some of the businesses, including Kahn Brothers Department Store, became regional giants. At the same time, men like Abraham Bercovich and Abraham Jonas served as civic leaders and formed the basis of religious life. In the 1890s and after, Jews from Eastern Europe settled in the city and formed a number of new, more observant synagogues. (First Hebrew, while it began as an Orthodox congregation, always had some liberal tendencies.)

After World War I, as the East Bay grew north into Berkeley (where the University of California was located), the Jewish population developed as well. In the aftermath of the war, the East Bay Federation was formed to respond to the needs of the ever-expanding population. After World War II, the community continued to expand, including new synagogues and institutions that spread east into Contra Costa County as well as north and south along the bay. In addition to the development of religious institutions of all kinds, the East Bay has become the home of numerous cultural organizations that have touched thousands of lives. It is safe to say that few, if any, regions in the country have formed such a varied group of associated events. They include, among others, the first Jewish film festival and the oldest Jewish music festival, both developed in the East Bay. In addition, the rabbinic community has created and supported events, from community high school programs and an annual Holocaust Memorial to regional Shavuot learning sessions, that cross denominational lines and truly create a sense of unity of purpose.

Thus, over almost a century and a half, the story of Jewish life in Oakland, Berkeley, and the entire East Bay reflects both the national saga of Jewish activities and individual stories that transcend the local. This book seeks to make these two stories visual and to demonstrate how they have served each other, making a vibrant tapestry in the early 21st century.

One

THE FOUNDERS' GENERATION
1865–1914

Santa Fe Depot · Oakland, California

Many cross-country travelers bound for San Francisco, from the 1860s until today, have ended their journey in Oakland. Until the construction of the Bay Bridge in the mid-1930s, they took ferries across the bay. This postcard image of the Santa Fe railroad depot might have been sent by new arrivals to the folks back home to indicate they had arrived in California. (Courtesy of the California Historical Society, FN-36633.)

The western half of the Transcontinental Railroad was built by the California Pacific Railroad and completed in 1868. The company built its Oakland station, the end of the line, in 1869. In order to accommodate the passengers and freight, and to develop the Port of Oakland as an alternative to San Francisco, the railroad built this enormous port facility, popularly known as "the Mole." (Courtesy of the California Historical Society, FN-36635.)

Parr Terminal

In addition to frequent service across the bay to San Francisco, there were daily ferries to Sacramento, Stockton, and other inland cities that readily accepted the new arrivals. Boat service to and from Sacramento lasted well into the 20th century. This 1921 photograph shows the busy port from the air. (Courtesy of the California Historical Society, FN-36632.)

Although Oakland was always overshadowed by San Francisco, it was never a "cow-town." When Gertrude Stein, who grew up there, said that "there is no *there* there," she greatly underestimated the city. It served at first as an entry point for Gold Rush pioneers who crossed San Francisco Bay, but after the arrival of the railroad in the 1870s, it grew more rapidly. This photograph from 1879 shows its emergence into a significant city. By the time of this photograph, First Hebrew Congregation was a thriving synagogue with its own building and a prosperous membership. (Courtesy of the California Historical Society, FN-36631.)

By the early 1860s, Oakland was in need of a cemetery site away from its growing downtown. A committee was chosen, and it decided on a location at the far end of Piedmont Avenue. The Mountain View Cemetery Association was formed in 1863 to develop the site. The cemetery was later laid out by the great landscape architect Frederick Law Olmstead. It has become a landmark in Oakland history, and it is the resting place for numerous significant Californians, including governors and other leaders. (Courtesy of the California Historical Society, FN-36634.)

In 1865, several Jewish Oaklanders, led by Alexander Hirshberg, Isador Alexander, and Jacob Letter, created a Jewish burial society. They purchased an area at the base of Mountain View Cemetery and named the Jewish section "Home of Eternity." In the 1880s, the cemetery became part of First Hebrew Congregation (now Temple Sinai). The synagogue still owns and operates the area separately from Mountain View. The mausoleum was first built in 1938 and has been expanded several times. (Author photograph.)

Born in Poland, Jacob Letter was one of the founders of Oakland's Jewish community. He was one of the purchasers of Home of Eternity cemetery in 1865 and was a founding member and president of First Hebrew Congregation. He died of a heart attack on the day of the dedication ceremony for the synagogue's second building in 1886. This is the headstone for his and his wife's grave in Home of Eternity Cemetery. (Author photograph.)

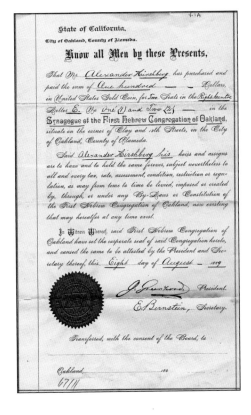

Along with Isador Alexander and Jacob Letter, the Hirshbergs were among the "first families" of Oakland Jewry. Samuel Hirshberg was among the first Jews in the city and was a founder of First Hebrew Congregation. His son David was the first Jew born in the city. Alexander Hirshberg was given this deed, possibly for a grave site, in 1889. (Courtesy of the Judah L. Magnes Museum/Western Jewish History Center, WJHC 1967-053-002.)

Soon after its formation in 1875, First Hebrew Congregation embarked on the construction of a synagogue. This drawing shows the front of the building at Fourteenth and Webster Streets. "FHC" (for First Hebrew Congregation) was engraved over the door. Like many synagogues of the time, including the Plum Street Temple in Cincinnati and Temple Emanu-El in San Francisco, the building had Moorish elements as primary design features. When the building was destroyed by fire in 1885, a brave congregant entered the burning sanctuary and saved the Torah scrolls. (Drawing by Ruth Eis, courtesy of Temple Sinai.)

In 1881, First Hebrew Congregation hired its first rabbi. Meyer Solomon Levy was raised in London but immigrated to Australia as a young man. Prior to coming to Oakland, he had been the rabbi in San Jose. A public-spirited man, he gave a portion of his monthly $100 salary to the poor. After fire destroyed the synagogue in 1885, he traveled up and down the West Coast collecting funds to rebuild. He was also a rigorous defender of Jewish principles. When the Oakland schools refused to excuse students on the High Holy Days, he petitioned the superintendent. The district agreed, and teachers were directed not to hold examinations on Jewish holidays. (Courtesy of Temple Sinai.)

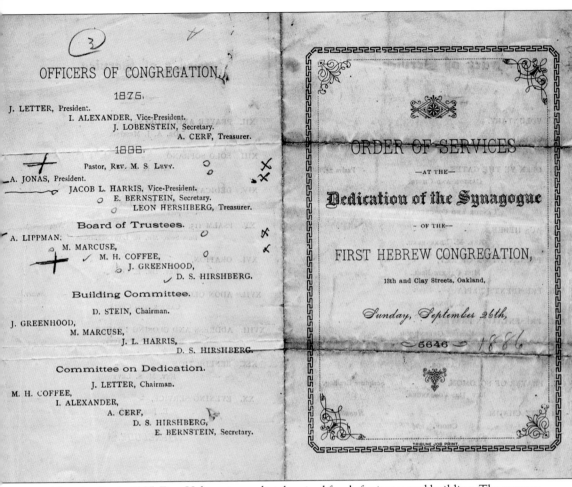

OFFICERS OF CONGREGATION.

1875.

J. LETTER, President.
I. ALEXANDER, Vice-President.
J. LOBENSTEIN, Secretary.
A. CERF, Treasurer.

1886.

Pastor, Rev. M. S. Levy.
A. JONAS, President.
JACOB L. HARRIS, Vice-President.
E. BERNSTEIN, Secretary.
LEON HERSHBERG, Treasurer.

Board of Trustees.

A. LIPPMAN,
M. MARCUSE,
M. H. COFFEE,
J. GREENHOOD,
D. S. HIRSHBERG.

Building Committee.

D. STEIN, Chairman.
J. GREENHOOD,
M. MARCUSE,
J. L. HARRIS,
D. S. HIRSHBERG.

Committee on Dedication.

J. LETTER, Chairman.
M. H. COFFEE,
I. ALEXANDER,
A. CERF,
D. S. HIRSHBERG,
E. BERNSTEIN, Secretary.

ORDER OF SERVICES

—AT THE—

Dedication of the Synagogue

— OF THE—

FIRST HEBREW CONGREGATION,

13th and Clay Streets, Oakland,

Sunday, September 26th,

5646 1886

TRIBUNE JOB PRINT.

After the fire in 1885, First Hebrew immediately raised funds for its second building. The women of the congregation held a "Grand Fair" that raised a significant amount, and Rabbi Levy also helped in the effort. A year after the disaster, the new building at Thirteenth and Clay Streets, with Moorish elements inspired by Isaac Mayer Wise's Plum Street Temple in Cincinnati, was dedicated. This is the cover of the dedication brochure. Tragically, Jacob Letter, one of the congregation's founders, suffered a heart attack and died on the day of the ceremony. (Courtesy of Temple Sinai.)

This photograph shows the home of First Hebrew as it was in 1900. In 1895, the structure was raised off its original foundations and moved a few blocks away to Twelfth and Castro Streets. (Courtesy of Temple Sinai.)

Endowment Declaration Book

OF

Oakland LODGE, NO. 252.

I, Jacob Letter a member of

Oakland Lodge, No. 252, INDEPENDENT ORDER

B'NAI B'RITH, do hereby declare that the amount of endowment which shall become due at my death shall be distributed as follows:

To Joseph Benny Letter of Oakland

the sum of One Thousand (1000) — dollars.

To Ida Letter of Oakland

the sum of One Thousand (1000.) — dollars.

To —— of

the sum of ____ dollars.

To ____ of

the sum of ____ dollars.

To ____ of

the sum of ____ dollars.

To ____ of

the sum of ____ dollars.

Signed this Third day of August 1886

Jacob Letter

E Bunstein Secretary.

Oakland's B'nai B'rith chapter held subscription drives to endow its various activities. These two pages are from its Endowment Book. Jacob Letter's page was written up only a few months before his death. Henry Kahn was a member of a family of store owners whose activities would benefit the city for the next 50 years. (Both courtesy of the Judah L. Magnes Museum/Western Jewish History Center.)

Endowment Declaration Book

OF

Oakland LODGE, NO. 252

I, Henry Kahn a member of

Oakland Lodge, No. 252, INDEPENDENT ORDER

B'NAI B'RITH, do hereby declare that the amount of endowment which shall become due at my death shall be distributed as follows:

To My Mother Mrs Israel Kahn of Oakland

the sum of Two Thousand dollars.

To ____ of

the sum of ____ dollars.

To ____ of

the sum of ____ dollars.

To ____ of

the sum of ____ dollars.

To ____ of

the sum of ____ dollars.

To ____ of

the sum of ____ dollars.

Signed this Apr 10th day of 1888

Henry Kahn

E Bunstein Secretary.

David Magnes left Poland in 1863 and arrived in San Francisco by way of Panama. He married Sophie Abrahamson, who came from Posen in Polish Germany. The couple moved to Oakland, where they ran a successful dry goods store. This photograph was taken around 1877, when their son Judah was born. (Courtesy of the Judah L. Magnes Museum/Western Jewish History Center, WJHC 1968-030-013.)

Judah Leon Magnes was raised in Oakland. After bar mitzvah at First Hebrew Congregation, he continued his Jewish education, studying with Rabbi Jacob Voorsanger at Temple Emanu-El in San Francisco. Magnes attended Hebrew Union College in Cincinnati and served as a rabbi in New York, where he was instrumental in creating the Kehillah, a mutual aid organization for immigrant Jews on the Lower East Side. Magnes immigrated to Palestine after World War I. He later became the first president of the Hebrew University of Jerusalem and oversaw its development until his death in 1948. (Courtesy of the Judah L. Magnes Museum/Western Jewish History Center, WJHC 1968-030-002.)

CONGRATULATIONS

by WESTERN UNION

FAB724 10 SC=CHAMPAIGN ILL

1940 NOV 15 PM 7 13

WM M STERN=

    1ST HEBREW CONGREGATION 28TH AND WEBSTER=

CONGRATULATIONS AND BEST WISHES ON 65TH ANNIVERSARY FOR
SINAI CONGRETGATION=
    RAY FRANK LITMAN.

As a teenager in the 1880s, Rachel Frank lived in Oakland and served as First Hebrew's religious school principal. A few years later, while living in Portland, Oregon, she delivered a stirring High Holy Day sermon, becoming the first American Jewish woman to speak from a pulpit. The event was reported in the national Jewish press, and she became known as the "Girl Rabbi of the West" for her accomplishment. For several years thereafter, she was a powerful lecturer on Jewish topics, speaking in towns and cities across the country. Isaac Mayer Wise even invited her to attend classes at Hebrew Union College in Cincinnati. She sent this telegram to help commemorate Temple Sinai's 65th anniversary in 1930. (Courtesy of Temple Sinai.)

German-born Rabbi Marcus Friedlander was hired by First Hebrew Congregation in 1893 and remained its spiritual leader until 1918. A cautious reformer, he brought the synagogue into the Union of American Hebrew Congregations (the Reform movement's organization), and adopted the Union Prayer Book. Under his guidance, the congregation became a force within the community. After the San Francisco earthquake and fire in April 1906, First Hebrew became a temporary sanctuary for victims. As the synagogue grew, he was the driving force behind the construction of its elegant building at Twenty-eighth and Webster Streets. (Courtesy of the Judah L. Magnes Museum/Western Jewish History Center, from the *Emanu-El Magazine*.)

When the University of California moved from Oakland to Berkeley in 1870, the first building on the new campus was South Hall. It has served many purposes over the past 140 years. One of the first Jewish students on campus was Fannie Bernstein, who graduated in 1882. In the 1890s, a donation of over 1,000 books was made to the university library by a Mr. Greenebaum. (Author photograph.)

From 1889 until his death in 1908, Jacob Voorsanger was the spiritual leader of Temple Emanu-El in San Francisco. In addition to his formal rabbinate, he served as mentor to young Judah Magnes. In 1894, Voorsanger created the Semitics department at the University of California. It was one of the first Middle East study programs in America and the first in the west. (Courtesy of the Judah L. Magnes Museum/Western Jewish History Center, from the *Emanu-El Magazine*, vol. 25, no. 25, p. 2.)

Within a generation of its beginning, Oakland's Jewish community had a wide range of organized groups. The photograph on the right presents the young men who ran the early Young Men's Hebrew Association (YMHA). The YMHA probably operated in rented space at that time. There was also a Hebrew Women's Benevolent Society closely associated with First Hebrew Congregation. Oakland's first Jewish Community Center building was constructed on Brush Street (near the current Highway 980-880 intersection) in 1914. Below is a group on a weekend outing. (Both courtesy of the Judah L. Magnes Museum/ Western Jewish History Center.)

At the beginning of the 20th century, Oakland's Jews formed a number of organizations. While the assimilated German Jews joined the local B'nai B'rith lodge, the Ostjuden, recent immigrants from Eastern Europe and Russia, created a new social group for young people that they named "the Judaeans." Primarily a social group, it grew to over 150 members. Activities included outings to the country and picnics along Lake Merritt, a few blocks from home. (Both courtesy of the Judah L. Magnes Museum/Western Jewish History Center WJHC, 1967-011-003_001, 1967-011-005_001.)

PROGRAM *at the* LAYING OF THE CORNER STONE *of the*

Beth-Jacob Congregation

A. MERRILL BOWSER, ARCHITECT

| Sunday, June 2nd 1907 | The 20th of Sivan 5667 |

NINTH AND CASTRO STS.

| OAKLAND | CALIFORNIA |

Between the 1880s and World War I, millions of Jews emigrated from Russia and Eastern Europe and settled in the United States. Several thousand of them came to Oakland and settled in the old downtown area near the foot of Broadway. In 1893, a new synagogue, Congregation Beth Jacob, was formed. While the majority of the city's Jews moved away from downtown over the succeeding years, Beth Jacob remained near its original site for over 50 years. The congregation's rabbi from 1922 until 1940 was B. M. Paper. In addition to his synagogue duties, during the Depression, Rabbi Paper also distributed kosher wine under a license allowing the sale of liquor for sacramental purposes. This is the cover of the program for the dedication of its synagogue. (Courtesy of Beth Jacob Congregation.)

After arriving from Europe in the 1880s, Abraham Bercovich became a successful scrap metal dealer in Oakland. Here he is shown with his wife, Bertha, and several of their children. Abraham Bercovich died in 1904. (Courtesy of Temple Beth Abraham.)

In 1906, after his father Abraham's death, Edward Bercovich opened a furniture store in downtown Oakland. The business thrived and became one of the primary sources for quality furnishings in the Bay Area. In the 1930s, the store began the practice of sponsoring sports teams. Edward died in 1938. This photograph, taken around 1914, shows Edward and his wife, Jenny, with some of their children. (Courtesy of Sam Bercovich.)

The First Pulpit of Temple Beth Abraham

Standing left to right: M. Jacobvitz, A. Gardner, Judel Gold (still a Temple member)
R. Gardner, two unknown gentlemen, M. Lipkin, president.

Around 1907, a group of Eastern European Jews split from Beth Jacob and incorporated a new synagogue. It was first known as the "Hungarian Shul" to distinguish it from the other Orthodox congregations and from the Reform First Hebrew Congregation. The community located a building near the foot of Harrison Street that they hoped to transform into a sanctuary. In order to purchase the structure, Bertha Bercovich donated a substantial gift. In appreciation, the synagogue took on the name of her late husband, and Temple Beth Abraham was born. This undated photograph shows the bima of the Harrison Street synagogue. (Courtesy of Temple Beth Abraham.)

As Eastern European immigrants arrived in Oakland, they established their own institutions. Because Home of Eternity Cemetery was associated with the liberal (Reform) world of First Hebrew Congregation, the Orthodox community decided to create a new cemetery. Home of Peace Cemetery was established around 1900 south of downtown near High Street. In 1926, a fountain was installed with the names of prominent members of the community inscribed on mosaic tiles around the base. The cemetery is still in use as the primary resting place for the East Bay's Orthodox community. (Author photographs.)

From 1860 until 1890, Isaias Hellman (center) was one of the leading bankers and entrepreneurs who were instrumental in the growth of Los Angeles and the California dream. In the 1890s, he moved his empire to San Francisco, where he became a leader in the creation of Wells Fargo Bank. He is shown with his family. (Courtesy of Dunsmuir Hellman Historic Estate.)

In early 1906, Marco Hellman, the son of banker Isaias Hellman, purchased the Dunsmuir House in the Oakland Hills from its original owners. The elegant mansion became the family's home when they were forced to leave San Francisco after the earthquake and fire of April 1906. Though most San Franciscans lived in tents during the months after the disaster, a significant number moved to Oakland and Berkeley. Many institutions, including First Hebrew Congregation, opened their doors to the refugees. The Hellman family continued to use the estate as a summer and weekend retreat until the late 1950s. (Courtesy of Dunsmuir Hellman Historic Estate.)

Among the many successful Jewish immigrants in Oakland, Jacob Pantoskey (right) stood out. He had come to California as a child and remained the community's "bad boy" throughout his life. He was a creative entrepreneur and owned several businesses in the region, but he always rejected propriety. He resisted union labor and kept his businesses open as long as the customers came. Despite thumbing his nose at almost all of "polite" society, however, he belonged to First Hebrew Congregation and attended his son's bar mitzvah there. (Courtesy of the Judah L. Magnes Museum/Western Jewish History Center WJHC-1975-003-002.)

Jacob Pantoskey's greatest accomplishment was leasing a group of retail stalls in downtown Oakland, near the foot of Broadway at Fifth and Washington Streets. He took responsibility for sanitation and advertising. The Free Market was successful, drawing customers from around the city, and was one of the only buildings in Oakland open six days a week, offering convenience and bargain prices. The first market was destroyed by the 1906 earthquake. A few years later, Pantoskey moved his operation to Tenth and Clay Streets, a block from Broadway and near the hub of downtown. Pantoskey, however, remained true to his image. He was once sued by inmates at the nearby Oakland city jail because of the loud music he played constantly in the market. (Both courtesy of the Judah L. Magnes Museum/ Western Jewish History Center, WJHC-1975-003-004, 003-001.)

Two

THE AGE OF MERCHANTS AND INSTITUTIONS
1914–1965

In the first part of the 20th century, Abraham Jonas was the quintessential public man in Oakland. As a business owner, he ran the Hub, a chain of successful department stores. As a public-minded citizen, he filled numerous public roles in the city of Oakland, though he lost his only bid for elective office. He served as president of First Hebrew Congregation from 1908 to 1918, a period that included the construction of its new home on Twenty-eighth Street. In 1921, a plaque was mounted in the synagogue's lobby attesting to his life's work. (Courtesy of the Judah L. Magnes Museum/Western Jewish History Center, WJHC 1970-008-001.)

Abraham Jonas's commitment to public service was epitomized by his desire for the unification of the East Bay's many towns into a single entity, metropolitan Oakland. He believed that regionalization would increase the city's importance and also provide services more efficiently. One of his ideas was to provide an improved connection between Oakland and Contra Costa County. Though Jonas died in 1923, his dream was fulfilled with the opening of the Caldecott Tunnel in 1937. The tunnel is now a California Landmark. (Author photograph.)

Architect Gustave Albert Landsburgh was raised in San Francisco and worked for Bernard Maybeck while attending the University of California. One of his first jobs in San Francisco was the rebuilding of Temple Emanu-El, which had been destroyed in the earthquake and fire of 1906. In 1913, he was hired to design the new home of First Hebrew Congregation in Oakland. His later commissions included the Orpheum Theater and the War Memorial Opera House in San Francisco and the Martin Beck Theater in New York. (Courtesy of the Judah L. Magnes Museum/Western Jewish History Center.)

In the early 1910s, First Hebrew Congregation found a new home on Twenty-eighth Street between Summit and Webster Streets just off Broadway. The ground-breaking took place on October 26, 1913 and Temple Sinai was dedicated a year later. This 1920s exterior view shows the front and side. Above the entry are the words "My House Shall Be a House of Prayer for All Peoples." The sanctuary was constructed along classical Reform synagogue lines, with a large pipe organ and a high bima. Six tall stained-glass windows on the sides represented primary Jewish values. The building also included a social hall and several classrooms. (Courtesy of the Judah L. Magnes Museum/Western Jewish History Center, from the *Emanu-El Magazine*, vol. 38, no. 20, p. 18.)

Israel Kahn, another of the great commercial and civic leaders of Oakland, emigrated from Germany to New York in 1848. In 1877, he and his family moved to San Francisco and then to Oakland. The family clothing business prospered for three generations under family leadership, especially under Israel. In 1912, Kahn Brothers' Department Store opened its elegant new store across the street from the new city hall. Designed by architect Charles Dickey, it featured a 120-foot-high atrium and a 5,000-square-foot domed ceiling. The building also had a parking lot next door, a major innovation in the early days of the automobile. The Rotunda, as it is known, was renovated in the 1990s and is now operated as a business center. (Left, courtesy of John F. Sampson and Jenny Sampson; below, author photograph.)

When Frederick Kahn died in 1929, his will provided for his heirs to establish an organization to serve public needs. One of the first major projects of the Kahn Foundation was the establishment of the East Bay Regional Park District for Alameda and Contra Costa Counties. By 2007, the park system had grown to encompass 65 units covering over 98,000 acres. They include recreation areas, historic sites, and over 1,150 miles of trails. (Author photographs.)

The Coffee family was another of the founding clans in Jewish Oakland. Michael Coffee was a clothing merchant and an early member of First Hebrew Congregation. His son Rudolph was raised in the synagogue, attended Columbia University, and was ordained a rabbi at the Jewish Theological Seminary in New York. After spending several years in the East and Midwest, Rabbi Coffee returned to Oakland as leader of Temple Sinai in 1921. During his 12-year term, he spoke eloquently about moral and social issues, including disarmament, Prohibition, and especially prison reform. (Courtesy of the Judah L. Magnes Museum/Western Jewish History Center, from the *Emanu-El Magazine*, vol. 65, no. 23, p. 11, Eman-065-023-011.)

BLAKE BLOCK.

In addition to the many Jewish-owned dry goods and clothing stores, H. C. Capwell's Lace House was a favorite shopping destination. Begun as a specialty shop for women, it expanded to a staff of over 800 people in 1912. The enormous Capwell's store on Clay and Fourteenth Streets had a restaurant, a childcare center, and home delivery of merchandise. This postcard suggests its elegance at the beginning of the 20th century. (Courtesy of the Judah L. Magnes Museum/Western Jewish History Center WHC 2000-001-001_001.)

Born in Sacramento, Albert S. Lavenson moved to Oakland and joined the staff of the Lace House in 1892. He rose to become a partner and vice president of the firm. A superb marketer for the store, Lavenson was also successful in marriage. His wife was a daughter of Isador Kahn; therefore, Frederick Kahn, the operator of Oakland's other great store, was Lavenson's brother-in-law. Kahn and Lavenson served as presidents of Temple Sinai in the mid-1920s. (Courtesy of the Judah L. Magnes Museum/Western Jewish History Center, from the *Emanu-El Magazine*, vol. 38, no. 20, p. 19, Eman-038-020-19_002.)

As more Jewish students attended college in the early 1900s, they needed an organization to support them and to provide both social services and religious community. In the 1910s, B'nai B'rith formed Hillel to assist and nurture Jewish students on college campuses across the country. In 1921, Rabbi Benjamin Goldstein was hired as the first Hillel director at the University of California at Berkeley. (Courtesy of the Judah L. Magnes Museum/ Western Jewish History Center, from the *Emanu-El Magazine*, vol. 65, no. 23, p. 50, Eman-065-023-050.)

From the time it was bought in the late 1920s until the construction of a new Hillel center in the 1990s, this was the focal point of Jewish student life on campus. (Courtesy of the Judah L. Magnes Museum/Western Jewish History Center, WJHC 1995-006-001.)

In the early 1900s, Jewish communities across the nation created centralized organizations to oversee the many programs that had sprung up. Oakland established the Jewish Welfare Federation after World War I. From the beginning, the agency was well supported. Its first president was Frederick Kahn, who put his authority and money behind it. This photograph shows the federation's office in the early 1920s in a building on Broadway. (Courtesy of the Judah L. Magnes Museum/Western Jewish History Center. WJHC 1967-011-008.)

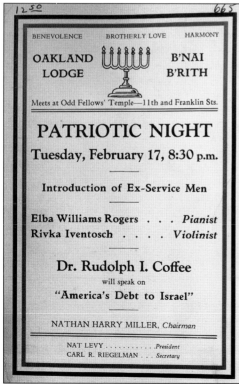

World War I brought out patriotic sentiment in Oakland's Jews. This flyer advertising a B'nai B'rith event was probably posted after America entered the war in 1917. It is likely that the evening drew a sizable audience. The members would have heard a speaker (either a performer or a local) talking about the destruction of Western Europe by the German army and the need to support American troops. These Four Minute Men would have concluded their comments by urging the audience to purchase war bonds as a way to "Help Defeat the Kaiser." (Courtesy of the Judah L. Magnes Museum/Western Jewish History Center. WJHC 1967-001-001.)

In the mid-1920s, Samuel Kohs served as executive director of the Oakland Jewish Welfare Federation. He later rose to prominence on the national stage of American Jewish communal service and became a vocal critic of the existing mode of operation by communal organizations. He noted, for example, that many small groups resisted regional unification in favor of local pride, even when the benefits of cooperation were obvious. While leading the Brooklyn Federation in the 1930s, he helped merge that organization with the Manhattan group, leading to a New York City–wide Federation of Jewish philanthropies. (Courtesy of the Judah L. Magnes Museum/ Western Jewish History Center. WJHC 1967-011-027.)

For over 30 years, from 1926 until 1959, the East Bay Federation's executive director was Harry Sapper (right). Under his leadership, the community moved from having almost exclusively local interests to developing a wider view of the world. In this photograph, Sapper is seen presenting an award. (Courtesy of the Judah L. Magnes Museum/Western Jewish History Center, WJHC 1967-011-026.)

The leadership of an organization speaks volumes about the people it represents. Over its 90-year history, the presidents of the East Bay Federation have come from across the spectrum of the community, including members of several synagogues and a variety of business backgrounds. Lionel Wachs (left) and Robert Fischer (below) both also served as presidents of Temple Sinai. (Both courtesy of the Judah L. Magnes Museum/ Western Jewish History Center: Lionel Wachs 1967-011-029; Robert Fischer 1967-011-030.)

Sam Clar and his family were prominent antique dealers in the Oakland area for many years. Sam served as president of the federation in 1957. (Courtesy of the Judah L. Magnes Museum/ Western Jewish History Center, WJHC 1967-011-028.)

In Oakland, as in most cities, the federation divided its responsibilities among working groups. One of the primary fund-raising activities was an annual dinner to celebrate successes during the past year and to generate enthusiasm for the next year's programs. This photograph was taken at the 1935 meeting of the East Bay Federation's Junior Division. (Courtesy of the Judah L. Magnes Museum/Western Jewish History Center, WJHC 1967-011-015.)

In 1909, the first synagogue in Berkeley was founded. Named Congregation Beth Israel, it was Orthodox. The synagogue they constructed in the 1920s was on Bancroft Street, about a mile from the University of California campus. For many years, services were held only a few times a year, and there was no rabbi. This photograph shows the Silver Anniversary Dinner, held in 1949. (Courtesy of June Safran.)

By the late 1920s, much of the Jewish community had moved away from downtown Oakland. In addition, the installation of the new tunnel between the cities of Oakland and Alameda (known as the Posey Tubes) required that Temple Beth Abraham abandon its original home on Harrison Street. As a result of its displacement, Beth Abraham found a new location near Lake Merritt and constructed a grand new edifice. The new sanctuary had family pews rather than a division between men's and women's seating areas. Soon after, the synagogue hired its first fulltime rabbi, Moses Goldberg. Also at that time, the congregation moved away from Orthodoxy and declared itself Traditional Conservative. (Courtesy of Temple Beth Abraham.)

This photograph shows the grand interior of Beth Abraham when it opened in 1929. This photograph was taken at the service dedicating a new Torah scroll acquired in 1930. (Courtesy of Temple Beth Abraham.)

Edward Bercovich's son Sam joined his father's furniture business and continued its success for 40 years. In addition, Sam inherited his father's passionate commitment to the underdog. Beginning in the 1930s, the family sponsored and supported numerous sports teams and especially African American athletes. Throughout his life, Sam dedicated himself to giving others the opportunity to thrive, both on the field and in life. In the 1960s, he was an early investor in the Oakland Raiders. In this 2009 photograph, 92-year old Sam, still an active member of Beth Abraham, regales visitors with stories about his long life in Oakland. (Author photograph.)

In the early 20th century, Harry Edmonds became concerned about international communication, particularly among college students. In the late 1920s, he convinced John D. Rockefeller to establish a series of international houses on university campuses around the nation. Their purpose was to foster international understanding by creating living and communal space for students and visiting scholars from around the world. The International House in Berkeley, with its distinctive domed tower, opened in 1930. Over the past 80 years, the building has been home to a wide range of foreign students and visiting scholars, including many important Jews from around the world. (Author photograph.)

One of the highlights of December every year is the celebration of Hanukkah, the Festival of Lights. In 1945, the end of World War II and prospects for a Jewish state in Palestine made the celebration especially memorable and poignant. This invitation was for the annual event at U.C. Berkeley's Hillel. (Courtesy of the Judah L. Magnes Museum/Western Jewish History Center, WJHC 1970-010-001.)

B'NAI B'RITH
Hillel Foundation
2727 channing way

announces_____

Festival
of
HANUKKAH

Sunday_Dec. 17th._at_8:30 pm
THERE WILL BE *LATKAHS* AND *FUN*
AND *DANCING* AND MUCH MORE_

EVERYONE WELCOME   ADMISSION 25¢

While Oakland's federation was not immediately successful in its early attempts to raise money, the organization gained strength after World War II. Its 1946 campaign exceeded its ambitious $375,000 goal. Among its aims was the resettlement of Jewish displaced persons who had survived the Holocaust and support of Jews in the Holy Land that would soon become Israel. It is especially notable that not all the money came from Jewish sources. According to this article in the *Welfare Federation News*, a local Catholic priest made an appeal at a boxing match that brought in "more than $3,900." The campaign also was supported by the Oakland Chamber of Commerce and the University of California. (Courtesy of the Jewish Federation of the Greater East Bay.)

Another group vital to the federation's success in Oakland and elsewhere through the generations has been the Women's Division. This photograph was taken at a women's campaign meeting during the 1947-1948 campaign. (Courtesy of the Judah L. Magnes Museum/Western Jewish History Center, WJHC 1967-011-017.)

William Stern (far right) was born in Austria, but his parents immigrated to San Francisco soon after. He came under the influence of Rabbi Martin Meyer of Temple Emanu-El as a boy and left home as a teenager to attend the University of Cincinnati and Hebrew Union College, where he was ordained. After several years in the Midwest, he and his wife, Rae, arrived in Oakland in 1934. During his 31 years as Temple Sinai's spiritual leader, he became a fixture in the community. This photograph, probably taken in the 1950s, shows his connection to all levels of the synagogue. Longtime congregants recalled that he would stand outside the doors on Sunday mornings and greet each religious school child by name. (Courtesy of the Judah L. Magnes Museum/Western Jewish History Center WJHC 1967-053-004.)

Oakland created its Home for Jewish Parents after World War II. The photograph above was taken at the ground-breaking for the facility in 1950. It provided an important connection for elders for almost half a century, until the opening of the Reutlinger Center for Jewish Living. The photograph below shows the Jewish home's solarium in 1970. The open setting was an important feature of the building and drew people every day. (Both courtesy of the Judah L. Magnes Museum/Western Jewish History Center: above, WJHC 1967-011-022; below, WJHC 1967-011-021.)

Hungarian Jewish refugees show Harry J. Sapper two close friends pictured in line-up at Joint Distribution Committee in Vienna. Newcomers shown were interviewed by social workers in Federation's Family Service office. This emphasizes how desperate is the need to help over 100,000 new Jewish refugees now.

Temple Beth Abraham began its life as a synagogue focused on the Eastern European immigrant community. Over time, it became Americanized, and it has served as Oakland's Conservative congregation for many years. In the mid-1950s, the Hungarian Revolution and its aftermath brought an influx of refugees to Oakland. They were welcomed by the synagogue and its members. This 1957 photograph shows Harry Sapper of the East Bay federation welcoming one family group. From left to right are George Tabak, Lidia Mandel, Harry Sapper, Eva Fulop, and Thomas Tabak. (Courtesy of Lisa Tabak.)

In 1959, Beth Abraham celebrated its golden jubilee and also its 30th anniversary in its building on MacArthur Boulevard. This is the journal the synagogue issued to commemorate the event. (Courtesy of the Judah L. Magnes Museum/Western Jewish History Center, WJHC 1973-011-001.)

During his 31 years as leader of Temple Sinai, Rabbi William Stern became a community leader. Among his duties were service as a fire department chaplain (for which he received a fire hat), involvement in B'nai B'rith, and commitment to social and religious issues. This photograph shows him in 1963 receiving a certificate of merit. (Courtesy of the Judah L. Magnes Museum/Western Jewish History Center, WJHC 1967-011-023.)

This portrait shows Rabbi Stern with his wife, Rae, in 1963. While the rabbi was recognized for his many activities both within and outside the congregation, Rae Stern was also a powerful force at Temple Sinai. She taught in the religious school, led the synagogue's sisterhood, and served as a model for the congregation. An award for service to the synagogue was created in her honor and is presented by the Temple Sinai Sisterhood. (Courtesy of Temple Sinai.)

During World War II, more Jews began settling "over the hills" and through the Caldecott Tunnel in Contra Costa County. In 1951, a new chapter of the League of Jewish Women was formed. Those families later formed a new synagogue, holding religious school classes at the Lafayette Town Hall and Sabbath services in a church in Walnut Creek. In 1953, the new community, called Temple Isaiah, purchased this building, a Polynesian-themed restaurant and nightclub next to the freeway in Lafayette. The synagogue used the building as its sanctuary with changes occurring over time. The congregation hired its first rabbi in 1955 and its first part-time cantor in 1959. On its 50th anniversary in 2002, Temple Isaiah was the largest synagogue in the East Bay and an active participant in East Bay Jewish life. (Courtesy of the Judah L. Magnes Museum/ Western Jewish History Center, WJHC 977-017-001.)

The photograph to the right shows members of Temple Isaiah constructing the community sukkah in the early 1960s. (Courtesy of Temple Isaiah.)

Rabbi Shelley Waldenberg led Temple Isaiah from 1972 until 1991, providing the young synagogue with stability and warmth. (Courtesy of Temple Isaiah.)

ק"ק בני שלום

CONGREGATION B'nai shalom

74 ECKLEY LANE • WALNUT CREEK, CALIFORNIA 94596 • (415) 934-9446
GORDON M. FREEMAN, RABBI

During World War II, the East Bay population grew as wartime workers and their families worked at the expanded shipyards in Concord and Martinez. After the war, a number of Jews in Concord felt the need for a synagogue. As a result, a small congregation was formed. In the 1960s, the synagogue moved to the growing city of Walnut Creek, where it expanded to become Congregation B'nai Shalom. Its building complex near downtown was completed in the early 1980s. Under the 38-year rabbinate of Rabbi Gordon Freeman, the community became the center of Conservative Jewry in Contra Costa County. (Courtesy of B'nai Shalom Congregation.)

A MESSAGE FROM *RABBI FREEMAN*

Our plans and dreams as a community are being fulfilled before our eyes as we watch the construction of our new Sanctuary and School facilities. As we continue to maintain our obligations we can expect our goals as a Kehilah K'dosha, a Sacred Community, to be met.

This Ad book - Calendar demonstrates the combined efforts of individuals meeting their obligations to our community. May their efforts be blessed with sweetness and satisfaction.

May our hopes be fulfilled during the New Year.

My family and I wish each of you a Shana Tova U'metuka - A good and sweet New Year.

Rabbi Gordon M. Freeman

In 1944, a group of friends and neighbors in North Berkeley created that city's second synagogue, Congregation Beth El. It was formed as an alternative to Congregation Beth Israel, which was Orthodox. Its first spiritual leader was Rabbi Joseph Gitin, director of the University of California Hillel. In 1950, the congregation purchased land for a synagogue in a residential neighborhood near Shattuck Avenue and Rose Street. The synagogue also created Camp Kee Tov, an innovative summer program that integrated camping with Jewish learning. When the synagogue moved a few blocks away in 2005, it sold the building to the Graduate Theological Union. (Author photograph.)

In 1947, Temple Sinai expanded its facility, adding a school and office wing and a chapel. The synagogue's entrance moved around the corner to Summit Street. This photograph was taken at the ground-breaking; Rabbi William Stern can be seen in the dark suit at the right of the group. (Courtesy of Temple Sinai.)

From 1952 until 1970, Rabbi Harold Schulweis (seen here dancing with his wife) was Temple Beth Abraham's spiritual leader. A forceful speaker, Rabbi Schulweis was an advocate of women's equality in Jewish ritual matters and encouraged a broadening of women's responsibility within the synagogue. He also supported the civil rights movement and spoke out against the mistreatment of African Americans in Oakland and around the nation. (Courtesy of Temple Beth Abraham.)

For many years, the primary East Bay Federation event was a gala dinner. The photograph above was taken during the event in 1955. Below is a photograph of four unidentified leaders of the Women's Division in 1954. (Both courtesy of the Jewish Community Federation of the Greater East Bay.)

As part of the annual federation campaigns, brochures and fliers were routinely sent to workers and contributors. This 1957 brochure highlights the effort to raise $100,000 for the federation's many activities. (Courtesy of Aaron and Frances Greenberg.)

Oakland's first Jewish Community Center (JCC), near downtown on Brush Street, was built in 1914 and thrived for over 40 years as a gathering place. It was a home for theatrical productions, athletics, and numerous other activities, bringing all Jews together for recreation and entertainment. After World War II, however, the community center aged, and its members continued to move into the hills and beyond. In 1955, a new JCC was constructed on Sheffield Avenue near Fruitvale. The building was in use for 35 years, until the late 1980s. This photograph was taken at the center's ground-breaking. (Courtesy of the Judah L. Magnes Museum/Western Jewish History Center, WJHC 1967-011-013.)

For over 130 years, the East Bay Jewish community has cared for its own members. The first organization was the Daughters of Israel Relief Society, which was founded in 1877. After the San Francisco earthquake and fire in 1906, refugees were ferried across the bay and housed in Oakland-area shelters, including the sanctuary of First Hebrew Congregation. The relief society became part of the Jewish Welfare Relief Federation in 1918 and became more professional while still serving the needy. In the 1930s, the social service arm of the federation was named the Family Welfare Committee, and in the 1950s, it was again renamed the Jewish Family Service of the Greater East Bay. The current name, Jewish Family and Children's Services, was adopted in 1993, and the agency regained its independence in 1996. Over the past 60 years, the agency has served Holocaust survivors, émigrés from Eastern Europe and the Soviet Union, and immigrant communities from across Europe and Asia. It currently provides mental health and social services to a broad spectrum of the needy in the East Bay. Its unique areas of expertise are in assisting émigrés acculturate to their new lives, planning for the aging process within families, and building family relationships. This photograph shows a board meeting, possibly in the 1960s. (Courtesy of Jewish Family and Children's Services of the East Bay.)

After over half a century in downtown Oakland, Congregation Beth Jacob built a new facility on Park Boulevard in the mid-1950s. Over the next 50 years, the community grew around the synagogue, creating a vibrant modern Orthodox neighborhood that has had a lasting impact on Oakland's Jewish life. (Author photograph.)

Beginning in the late 1950s, Congregation Beth Israel was revived as a new generation of younger, observant Jewish families moved to Berkeley. In the early 1960s, the synagogue hired its first fulltime rabbi, Saul Berman. He and his wife and their successors have created a dynamic Orthodox community in the city. Beth Israel participates in many communal activities, including an annual study session on Shavuot, which is held at the Jewish Community Center in North Berkeley. (Courtesy of June Safran.)

During the tumultuous era between 1955 and 1971, Rabbi Joseph Gumbiner (center) was the director of Berkeley Hillel. In addition to his work on campus during the time of the civil rights and free speech movements and the Vietnam War, he was a force on the national Jewish scene. Not content to remain in California during the mid-1960s, he also traveled to the South and worked for racial justice. (Courtesy of the Judah L. Magnes Museum/Western Jewish History Center, WJHC 1995-006-002.)

JEWS LIBERATE FEDERATION

From 11:30 a.m. on Friday, April 30 until 9:00 Saturday evening, over 45 members of the Jewish Education Coalition held a **Shabbat Sit-In** in the offices of the S.F. Jewish Welfare Federation. Our purpose was to protest the Federation's lack of response to the city's crisis in Jewish education. The sit-in represented the culmination of a series of attempts to reach the JWF through "legitimate channels" as well as the beginning of a mass movement, aimed at making the Federation responsive to the community's number one need – quality Jewish education.

In early April, the Berkeley Radical Jewish Union discovered that the survival of both Jewish day schools in San Francisco was in serious doubt. The Hebrew Academy was in grave financial trouble and had been requesting help from the Federation since early November, with no results. The Brandeis Day School was to be evicted from its premises at the end of the school year by the Bureau of Jewish Education (a Federation subsidiary), which owned the land and had different plans for it.

On April 13, the R.J.U. spoke to Federation officials, demanding that the predicaments of the two schools be alleviated and that a public debate be held, regarding the position of Jewish education in the list of Federation priorities. These demands were refused. The same day, we learned that the Hebrew Academy had been denied financial assistance by the Federation.

Our next step, on April 16, was to send a letter to the San Francisco Jewish Bulletin (another Federation subsidiary), which is the only substantial Jewish community newspaper in the city, inviting Federation's response. The letter was not answered and was refused publication. We later learned that because of its financial dependence upon Federation, the paper was reluctant to print a letter opposing Federation policy.

On April 25, we sent a letter directly to the Federation, expressing our disappointment with the Federation for ignoring both the crisis as well as our efforts to raise the issue. We called for an immediate reply to our proposals and stated that if such a response was not forthcoming, we would "proceed to make public, by any means at our disposal, all the evidence of the Federation's refusal to adequately educate its children."

On April 28, during a meeting of the R.J.U. to discuss the situation, we agreed that a Shabbat Sit-In was the best approach to dramatize the problem and effect change, and decided to expand into a coalition of various groups and individuals.

By Thursday evening, we had not received a reply from the Federation and decided to go ahead with our plans. By that time, S.F. Habonim,

Stanford Union of Jewish Students, Jewish Liberation Project and teachers from the area joined the Jewish Education Coalition. We re-stated the goals of our sit-in: 1) to impress the leadership of the JWF with the validity of our demands and the urgency of the situation, and 2) to catalyze support for our concerns from the Jewish community at large.

At 11:30 a.m. Friday morning, we reached the Mills Tower Building, unloaded our supplies, and brought them—food, song books, a *Torah* and portable ark, *siddurim*, Shabbat supplies, sleeping bags and extra clothes—all up to the sixth floor.

It could have been the main office of any American firm. Entering, we were greeted by a number of intent

MELVIN SWIG   THE CHEVRA
photo by V. Wong

bird-hunters, dressed in frontiersmen garb and frozen into seven Currier and Ives prints. Not one *mezuzah*, no Chagall or Ben Shahn. Nearby, an enormous thermometer showed us how much money had been collected for this year's campaign.

Singing Am Yisroel Chai, we handed out copies of the following statement to each Federation worker:

"Shabbat Shalom!
This is not a mere physical occupation.
Our intent is to present a peaceful demand for a re-evaluation of local funding priorities, especially in regard to Jewish Education. We hope to engage in meaningful discussion on these matters.
Later we plan to celebrate a traditional Shabbat here as an approach to what a positive Jewish identity might be.
—Jewish Education Coalition"

Some of the secretaries seemed amused, if not interested, but most of the executives were quite irritated. Continuing our tactic of "creative disruption" (singing, dancing, engaging Federation workers in discussion), we presented them copies of our 6 page press release. It outlined the background to the Sit-In, explained the constituency of the Jewish Education Coalition, made the point that we were concerned with local (not overseas) funds, stated the purpose of having Shabbat at the Federation, and listed our demands (see page 3).

At about 1 p.m., the top executives of the Federation, including Melvin Swig (president) and Louis Weintraub (executive vice-president), with typical Federation disrespect for real Jewish culture, tried to interrupt our singing near the switchboard. We encouraged their participation and sang a few more songs.

When we finished, Swig said that he had a lot to do, but he would be glad to meet with us at a later date to discuss our demands, insisting that he would not consider them "under duress".

We told Swig that our group as a whole had to discuss and respond to his proposal. After our caucus we made the following counter-proposal: all of us would go into the large conference room, but only a small group (six of us who were chosen as spokesmen) would be allowed to talk with representatives of the Federation. Swig agreed, we all filed into the Conference room, and discussion began.

We began by arguing that the Federation **must** respond to the community's most essential need—Jewish education—by placing it first on the Federation's list of local priorities. Swig replied that he had no power to determine budgetary figures, informing us that the JWF was "a private not a public organization," responsible solely to its donors. When challenged on this point, Swig told us that (of course!) the JWF is concerned with the community. Look at the community agencies that receive large sums of money from Federation. "Besides," he said, "here we are, listening to a small group from the community like you." Such was our introduction to the renowned Federation practice of double-talk.

Swig then went on to tell us that the function of Federation was to allocate money to Jewish agencies, not to educate. Education was the function of institutions such as the Bureau of Jewish Education and the Community Centers, both of which

(Continued on Page 4)

"You Said it, I Didn't"

EDITOR'S NOTE: The following quotes from Federation leaders were heard either during our talks at the **Shabbat** Sit-In or during our follow-up meetings. As one Federation worker put it, "We seem to have a different view of the Jew than they do."

"We're just as interested in Jewish education as you are. But how do you know that it's the answer to Jewish identity?"—Lloyd W. Dinkelspiel, Jr. (vice-president of the JWF)

(Response to the statement that "unless we have Jewish education, twenty years from now we won't have any Jews")
"Well, I'd have to contradict you on that. Jews have been for 5,000 years."—Melvin M. Swig.

"We give money—we don't give programming."—Louis Weintraub (executive vice-president of the JWF)

"If I understand you correctly, what you want to do is to create a religio-political group that never existed! What you want is

more of an ethnic group, and my reading of Jewish history is that any time we've become more ethnic, we've opened ourselves to destruction."—John H. Steinhart (chairman, executive committee)

"We're a country of mixed ethnic groups. What's going to happen when these groups consolidate?"—Louis Weintraub

"We are a private organization, responsible to our donors."—Melvin M. Swig

"A public debate is not a particularly orderly process for studying the TOTAL needs of the community."—John H. Steinhart

"We don't have to defend ourselves (re: JWF budgetary priorities) because we've done it in a democratic process."—Melvin M. Swig

"We're not in the field to tell the community what it means to be a Jew. Other Jewish groups are doing that.—Melvin M. Swig

"To be a Jew . . . is to work for Jewish organizations . . . such as the Jewish Welfare Federation."—Melvin M. Swig

---

Jewish Education Coalition
c/o Radical Jewish Union
300 Eshleman Hall
Berkeley, California 94704

Shalom!
I agree with your demands to the Federation and support your efforts to make Jewish education the number one priority of the Jewish community.
Please put me on your mailing list, so that I can be notified about future developments and activities.

(name)
(address)
(phone)

Mr. Melvin M. Swig
Mr. Louis Weintraub
Jewish Welfare Federation
220 Bush Street
Suite 645
S.F. California 94104

Sirs:
I wish to register my support of the Jewish Education Coalition and its demands to the JWF.
I strongly believe that Jewish education is basic to ALL of our community needs, and therefore, should be made the Federation's number one local priority.
Shalom.

(name)
(address)

During the 1960s and 1970s, U.C. Berkeley was considered one of the epicenters of student activism. Beginning with the free speech movement and continuing through the Vietnam era, Berkeley was the place to be for young radicals. In 1971, students from the university and elsewhere staged a sit-in at the headquarters of the San Francisco Federation. This page from *The Jewish Radical*, a monthly newspaper, discusses both the reasons for the demonstration and its outcome. (Courtesy of the Judah L. Magnes Museum/Western Jewish History Center, WJHC 2003-011-001.)

If there is an individual who has most changed the cultural landscape of the San Francisco Bay Area, Seymour Fromer may be that person. In the 1950s, he arrived in Oakland and became head of the East Bay Federation's educational programs. Along with his wife, Rebecca, he also became an avid collector of Jewish art and artifacts. In the early 1960s, the Fromers created the Judah L. Magnes Museum, the first independent Judaica museum in the nation. Under this cultural umbrella, Seymour and Rebecca Fromer have spent the past four decades supporting the growth of Jewish arts and learning, including the Jewish Film Festival, Lehrhaus Judaica, and numerous other groups. (Courtesy of Seymour Fromer and the Judah L. Magnes Museum/Western Jewish History Center.)

In the early 1960s, Seymour and Rebecca Fromer established the Judah L. Magnes Museum to house Jewish art and ritual objects. It quickly expanded its role and outgrew its first home in the Jewish Community Center. In 1964, the Fromers rented space on the second floor of the Parkway Theater on Park Boulevard in Oakland to display the growing collection. The museum remained in the theater for two years before moving to the Burke mansion on Russell Street in Berkeley. (Author photograph.)

Over the next 40 years, the Magnes Museum became one of the world's leading Judaica museums. It also serves as the northern headquarters of the Western Jewish History Center, a major collection of documents on the history of American Jewish life. In 2004, the museum purchased a building in downtown Berkeley near the public library that will become the new home of many of its exhibits. (Author photographs.)

Artist Ruth Eis moved to Oakland in the 1950s with her husband, Max. They became early supporters of the Magnes Museum, where Ruth also served as curator for many years. The couple collected Judaic artworks, and Ruth wrote several catalogs and articles on aspects of their personal collection. To the left, she is shown with a pair of *rimmonim* (Torah scroll crowns) that she donated to the restored synagogue in Mainz, Germany, in 1993. Below is a catalog of an exhibit she curated for the Magnes Museum. (Both courtesy of Ruth Eis.)

ORNAMENTED BAGS
FOR TALLIT AND TEFILLIN
of the
Judah L. Magnes
Museum
by Ruth Eis

Three

THE CREATIVE ERA
1965–2000

After the death of Rabbi William Stern in December 1965, Temple Sinai found its next spiritual leader in Cleveland. During his tenure in Oakland, Rabbi Samuel Broude fought for both racial justice and *tikkun olam* (repair of the world). He was also a committed Zionist and led the congregation through a generation of change. While many urban synagogues moved to the suburbs, Temple Sinai remained connected to downtown Oakland. (Courtesy of Temple Sinai.)

Since the time of Rabbi Marcus Friedlander, Temple Sinai has proudly taken part in activities that affect the East Bay community. In 1906, the synagogue sheltered victims of the San Francisco earthquake. During the 1940s and 1950s, Rabbi Stern quietly and forcefully stood for Oakland during difficult times. This photograph shows a meeting of interfaith clergy in the Temple Sinai library; Rabbi Samuel Broude stands at the center. In the 1990s and after, Rabbi Steven Chester continued this tradition. The synagogue was a leading member of the Oakland Coalition of Congregations and has actively created and supported numerous programs to improve life in Oakland and the East Bay. (Courtesy of Temple Sinai.)

In 1964, this was the East Bay Federation Women's Division's Campaign Luncheon brochure. That year, Aaron Greenberg was the president of the federation. (Courtesy of Aaron and Frances Greenberg.)

Both before and after World War II, the Jewish Community Federation Women's Guild and other groups took a leading role in the region's activities. One of these was the Magnes Museum. From left to right in this undated photograph, probably from the 1970s, Gaye Olden, guild president Marianne Friedman, Jeremy Potash, Ruth Eis, and Frances Greenberg look over a shoe. (Courtesy of the Jewish Community Federation of the Greater East Bay and the Judah L. Magnes Museum/Western Jewish History Center.)

THE CENTENNIAL CELEBRATION SERVICE

under the auspices of

THE FINE ARTS FOUNDATION
OF TEMPLE SINAI

Composed Especially for our Hundredth Anniversary
by

GERSHON KINGSLEY

Text from the New Prayer Book

Conducted by
JOSEPH LIEBLING

APRIL 11, 1975   IYAR 1, 5735

TEMPLE SINAI
Oakland, California

Rabbi Samuel G. Broude   Roland Elefant, *President*
Cantor David Unterman   Morris Henerson, *Executive Director*

For many years, Temple Sinai has hosted a wide array of cultural programs, including the annual Stern Lecture series in memory of Rabbi William Stern. There have also been numerous other speakers and performers. During its centennial in 1975, Temple Sinai published this brochure advertising its musical and other artistic activities for the year. The celebration included several concerts, lectures, and a celebration of the synagogue's history. (Courtesy of the Judah L. Magnes Museum/Western Jewish History Center, WJHC 1967-053-003.)

In the 1960s and 1970s, the University of California was at the center of many of the changes in American society and politics. In addition, students became more conscious of their Jewish roots and solidified their connections to Israel, especially after the Six-Day War in 1967. The group pictured here saw itself as a Jewish, pro-Zionist voice on the left and a progressive, critical voice in the Jewish community. (Courtesy of Prof. David Biale.)

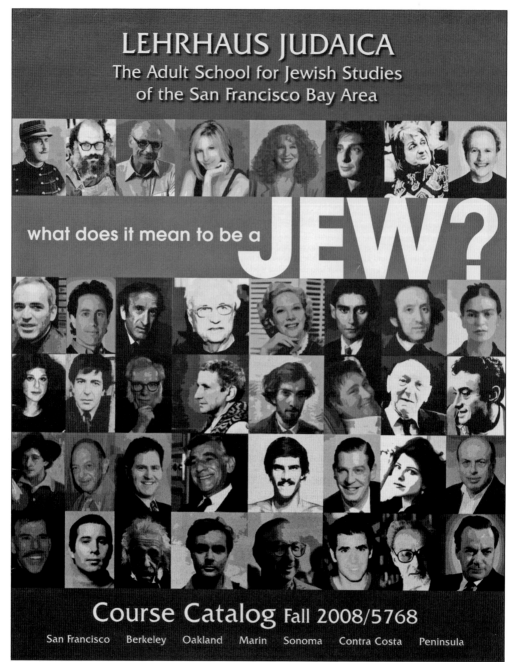

LEHRHAUS JUDAICA
The Adult School for Jewish Studies
of the San Francisco Bay Area

what does it mean to be a JEW?

Course Catalog Fall 2008/5768

San Francisco   Berkeley   Oakland   Marin   Sonoma   Contra Costa   Peninsula

In 1974, Fred Rosenbaum, a graduate student at the University of California, developed a new program of Jewish adult education with help from Rabbi Steven Robbins of Berkeley Hillel and the Magnes Museum's Seymour Fromer. Basing the organization on Franz Rosenzweig's 1920s school in Berlin, he created Lehrhaus Judaica. Over the years, Lehrhaus has held classes on Hebrew and Yiddish, history, and a wide variety of cultural topics. Lehrhaus has also sponsored several trips to New York, Europe, and Israel. Its fall 2008 catalog listed almost 80 classes at its home near the Berkeley campus and in over 30 other locations throughout the Bay Area. (Courtesy of Lehrhaus Judaica.)

This 1993 photograph shows Fred
Rosenbaum (left), founding director of
Lehrhaus Judaica, with Rabbi Alvin
Fine. (Courtesy of Lehrhaus Judaica.)

When Fred Rosenbaum decided to
pursue other professional interests, his
associate Jehon Grist succeeded him
as director of Lehrhaus. Under Grist's
guidance, the program has grown and
prospered. (Author photograph.)

In the mid-1970s, a group of parents in Berkeley founded Tehiyah ("renewal" in Hebrew), a non-sectarian Jewish day school. The group's intent was to develop a greater sense of commitment to Jewish life in the East Bay. In the mid-1980s, the school moved into a surplus elementary school in El Cerrito. Over the years, it has grown into a school from kindergarten through eighth grade that includes a strong general program and a solid Judaica curriculum. One of the daily events is *modeh ani*, the recital of the morning blessings before classes begin. The above photograph shows the school grounds from the street. (Author photograph.)

Since its inception in the 1970s, Tehiyah has blended Jewish learning and real-world experiences. In the process, the Jewish community has developed a new and strong generation of young and committed members. This photograph, taken in the school's early years, shows students studying a Torah scroll. (Courtesy of Tehiyah Day School.)

In the mid-1970s, the Chasidic group Chabad began sending emissaries around the nation. The intent was to reconnect unaffiliated Jews with, and ignite an interest in, Jewish learning and observance. One of the first Chabad Houses was established in Berkeley, and its leader was Rabbi Yehuda Ferris. For over 35 years, he has taught university students and others about the joys of Jewish observance. In addition, Berkeley Chabad differs from many Chabad centers in its interaction with rabbis and other Jewish institutions. One example is the annual overnight learning session on Shavuot. Above, Rabbi Ferris plays the guitar on Sukkot. Below is Chabad House, located on College Avenue in Berkeley. (Both courtesy of Rabbi Yehuda Ferris.)

As the Jewish population of the area moved beyond the Oakland-Berkeley hills in the 1960s and 1970s, the East Bay Federation also increased its services to them. One important addition to the community was the construction of a new Jewish Community Center in Walnut Creek in the late 1970s. This photograph shows a group of community leaders at the opening of the center. From left to right are Sue Ruttenberg, Barbara Kaplan, Lois Shainen, and Jim Carneman. (Photograph by Irwin Lazarus, courtesy of the Jewish Community Federation of the Greater East Bay.)

Since the mid-1980s, the federation has sponsored numerous cultural events at the Contra Costa JCC. One of the most popular is the Book Festival, held in the fall before Hanukkah. For more than 20 years, numerous writers, including some nationally known figures, have spoken about their books. In this 1989 photograph, Shirley Issel is the guest author. (Courtesy of the Contra Costa JCC.)

For some years, the Contra Costa Jewish Community Center was the central location for kosher Passover foods in the Contra Costa region. Here several women are shopping for goods. As the Jewish community grew, an increasing number of stores stocked kosher items, and the JCC stopped providing the service. (Courtesy of the Contra Costa JCC.)

The Contra Costa JCC has long prided itself on its preschool program, which includes creative dance, art, and other important activities for young children. This undated photograph shows a visit by the U.S. Forest Service, in the person of Woodsy Owl. (Courtesy of the Contra Costa JCC.)

In the early 1980s, the East Bay Federation took control of a 1910-vintage elementary school building in North Berkeley. Since that time, the Berkeley-Richmond Jewish Community Center has provided a wide variety of services for the local community. These include a preschool, lecture and educational space, and a small library. The JCC is a gathering place for many who have been alienated from synagogue connections but who wish to retain a connection to Jewish life and culture. (Author photograph.)

One of the special features of the Berkeley-Richmond JCC is its open-air courtyard. This photograph shows the 2003 Jewish Music Festival's Klezmer for Kids program, featuring Gerry Tenney and California Klezmer. (Courtesy of the Jewish Music Festival.)

Many people helped the federation achieve its goals during the 1970s. Above are the leaders involved in the teen campaign of 1979. Among the other participating groups were professionals, including doctors. (Courtesy of the Jewish Community Federation of the Greater East Bay.)

For over half a century, Aaron and Frances Greenberg have been vital members of Temple Sinai and the Bay Area Jewish community. Aaron served as president of Temple Sinai and of the Jewish Community Federation of the Greater East Bay and was an active member of B'nai B'rith and other organizations. Frances was involved in the Magnes Museum and served as the first female president of the federation from 1979 to 1981. This photograph was taken around 1980. (Courtesy of Aaron and Frances Greenberg.)

Beginning in the 1960s, the East Bay became a hotbed of experimental Jewish groups. These included the Aquarian Minyan, Kehilla Community Synagogue, and Chochmat HaLev. Rabbi Burt Jacobson was involved with several of them and was one of the guiding forces behind Kehilia when it was founded in the early 1980s. He also served as an advisor for many years. With its progressive politics and its insistence on inclusiveness, Kehilla continues to serve as a model for Renewal congregations around the nation. (Courtesy of Rabbi Burt Jacobson.)

Cody's Books, a Berkeley icon for 50 years, was founded in 1956 by Fred and Pat Cody and moved to Telegraph Avenue in 1967. In 1977, the Codys sold the store to Andrew Ross, who owned it until 2006. Among the legendary store's strengths was its long-running series of author readings and discussions, which crossed literary genres and styles. Another unique feature was its annual sale of Passover Haggadot (collected by Ira Steingroot), which included dozens of versions from across the spectrum of Jewish belief and around the world. Cody's flagship store closed in 2006; its last outlet shut its doors in 2008. (Author photograph.)

In 1981, the first independent Jewish film festival took place. Its creative director was Deborah Kaufman (left), an independent filmmaker who took the idea to Seymour Fromer at the Magnes Museum. The first year, 10 independent films were shown; the following year, Janis Plotkin (right) joined Kaufman as associate director. (Courtesy of Deborah Kaufman.)

By the 1990s, the Jewish Film Festival was invited to show films around the world. Deborah Kaufman and Janis Plotkin traveled to Russia in 1990 for the first Moscow Jewish Film Festival. On the left is Rustam Ibragimbekov, president of the Soviet Film Initiative; on the right is Roman Spektor, vice president of the Jewish Cultural Association. (Courtesy of Deborah Kaufman.)

In 1992, the 500th anniversary of the expulsion of the Jews from Spain, the Jewish Film Festival was invited to Madrid. (Courtesy of Deborah Kaufman.)

By 2008, the film festival had grown into a major Bay Area event. That year, over a three-week period, it presented 70 films from 19 countries around the world. Its 44 guests included filmmakers, subjects, and scholars, and it was attended by over 30,000 people. It remains the oldest and largest Jewish film event in the world. As in past years, the opening night was held at the magnificent Castro Theater in San Francisco. (Courtesy of the San Francisco Jewish Film Festival.)

In the 1970s, a new interest in ethnic music emerged from the folk revival and protest songs of the 1960s. Among the first groups to renew the tradition of Jewish music was the Klezmorim. Their first album, released in 1977, contained favorite tunes from the immigrant past on New York's Lower East Side, including "Yoshke Yoshke," "Sirbe/Hora" (a pair of dance tunes), and "Di Grine Kuzine" (the greenhorn cousin). Translations of several of the songs were printed on the album's back cover. (Courtesy of Arhoolie Records.)

As interest in Jewish music continued to grow in the Bay Area, Ursula Sherman saw an opportunity. She developed the Jewish Music Festival at the Berkeley-Richmond JCC in 1986. In 1998, Sherman invited her friend Eleanor Shapiro to codirect the event with her. One of the festival's inspirations came from the extensive collection of Jewish music compiled by Prof. Martin Schwartz of U.C. Berkeley. Ursula Sherman is at the center of this 2000 photograph, flanked by Martin Schwartz and Eleanor Shapiro. (Courtesy of Eleanor Shapiro, Jewish Music Festival.)

The first Jewish music festival in America took place in 1986. That one-day gathering in Berkeley became the model for numerous community festivals around the country. Over its long history, the festival has featured numerous Bay Area musicians, including Judy Frankel, the California Klezmer Band, Achi Ben Shalom, and Linda Hirschhorn and Vocolot. In addition, the festival has presented well-known national and international performers. Ruth Rubin, Daniel Hoffman, and Davka and Fran Avni have all taken part in the festival. In 2005, the 20th annual festival lasted over two weeks and included guests Theodore Bikel, the Omar Farouk Tikbilek Ensemble, and Joshua Nelson. Over the years, the festival has featured players and groups from around the world and styles as varied as contemporary Israeli, Dixieland, and Sephardic music. (Courtesy of the Jewish Music Festival.)

In the early 1950s, the Weavers helped create the groundwork for the revival of folk and ethnic music in America. Its most memorable voices were Ronnie Gilbert and Pete Seeger. Ronnie Gilbert appeared as guest of honor at the music festival in 2004. Here she is shown with JCC executive director Joel Bashevkin. (Courtesy of the Jewish Music Festival.)

After 23 years as spiritual leader of Temple Sinai, Rabbi Samuel Broude retired in 1989. His successor, Rabbi Steven Chester (above), took the programs that had grown up in the synagogue and expanded them dramatically. Over the next 20 years, the synagogue created a successful preschool, added adult education programs, and became even more deeply involved in community-building and tikkun olam at both the institutional and personal levels. Under Rabbi Chester, the synagogue grew to nearly 1,000 member families who saw the rabbi as a personal connection to Judaism and Jewish life. (Courtesy of Temple Sinai.)

Since the mid-1980s, Beth Jacob has been transformed into an energetic modern Orthodox community. Its rabbis, Howard Zack (above at right) and Judah Dardik (right), have taken significant places in the life of the greater community, including hosting community-wide events and serving actively on the regional Board of Rabbis. (Above, courtesy of Beth Jacob Congregation; right, author photograph.)

The Oakland Hills fire in October 1991 left thousands of people, including many Jewish families, homeless. The synagogues, led by their rabbis, helped them relocate and assisted many of the victims over the next year and beyond. One program collected household goods and clothes for the families and toys for the children. Here Temple Sinai's Rabbi Chester holds an armful of teddy bears collected for the children of the victims. (Photograph by Mel Silverman, courtesy of the Jewish Community Federation of the Greater East Bay.)

In the aftermath of the Oakland Hills fire, the East Bay Federation created a display to depict the devastation. In this photograph, Julie Moskowitz stands in front of a selection of newspapers, commentary, and objects pulled from the wreckage. (Photograph by Fred Speiser, courtesy of the Jewish Community Federation of the Greater East Bay.)

Over the years the East Bay Federation has also committed itself to many important programs to support refugees and immigrants from around the world. In the photograph above, Stanley Bass (right) of Jewish Family Services welcomes Sadrudin Esmail, a Ugandan refugee. In the 1980s, the Bay Area was a major center in the fight for refuseniks and became a destination for a number of Soviet émigrés. Also in the 1980s, Oakland took part in the relief effort to save and repatriate the Jews of Ethiopia. Below Gary Siepser, the Jewish Community Federation camp director, receives a check from Judith Brown. (Courtesy of the Jewish Community Federation of the Greater East Bay.)

In October 1991, Gerald Derblich (left) and David Cooper (right) opened Afikomen Judaica. Their store was the first in the East Bay to specialize in Judaica items. Afikomen stocked books, magazines, and music; Hanukkah menorahs and Passover seder plates; prayer shawls, jewelry, and artwork. The store thus provided a needed link between those who wished to learn more about Jewish life from a variety of perspectives and information in its numerous forms. In 2008, Chaim Mangel purchased the store. (Above, author photograph; below, courtesy of Gerald Derblich.)

In 1989, the Berkeley Conservative Congregation began holding Shabbat services in people's homes. In 1992, they renamed themselves Congregation Netivot Shalom ("Paths of Peace"). Under the leadership of Rabbi Stuart Kelman, the group became the city's Conservative synagogue, with its own unique participatory and egalitarian perspective. In 2005, Netivot Shalom moved into a new building on University Avenue near downtown Berkeley. The congregation remains very much lay-led under Rabbi Kelman's successor, Rabbi Menachem Creditor. (Both courtesy of Congregation Netivot Shalom.)

After an earlier career in the food business, Noah Alper opened the first Noah's Bagels on College Avenue in North Oakland in 1989. When he sold the business to Starbucks in 1995, there were over 35 Noah's in the region, and it was the largest kosher retailer in the nation. In 1999, he helped found the Jewish Community High School of the Bay, located in San Francisco, and served as its first president. In 2002, Noah and his wife, Hope, opened Ristorante Raphael, an Italian-themed kosher restaurant and caterer in downtown Berkeley. The Alpers also became significant contributors to numerous Jewish groups and activities throughout the East Bay. The primary theme of their activities is community. Their intent is to develop situations in synagogues, schools, or eating locations that encourage people to come together, find ways to communicate, and act on their beliefs. The photograph below was taken in front of the Western Wall in Jerusalem during the annual federation-sponsored summer trip to Israel for teenagers. That trip has taken place annually for over 25 years. (Both courtesy of Noah and Hope Alper.)

For many years, Joseph Zatkin and his family have played an integral role in East Bay Jewish activities. Joe Zatkin grew up in Oakland and played a significant role in the history of Temple Beth Abraham. He was also instrumental in the work of the East Bay Federation for many years and served as its president in the 1970s. Zatkin died in February 2009. (Courtesy of Temple Beth Abraham.)

For over 40 years, Michael Lerner has challenged American Jews' ways of thinking. As a graduate student at the University of California in the 1960s, he was involved in anti-Vietnam War activities and was a leader of the free speech movement. In 1986, he and Nan Fink founded *Tikkun* magazine, a voice of Jewish liberals and progressives. Since then, *Tikkun* has challenged the Jewish world to broaden its perspective. In 1995, Lerner was ordained a Renewal rabbi. In 2002, he created Beyt Tikkun in San Francisco, a community dedicated to understanding and peace. (Courtesy of *Tikkun* magazine.)

Born in 1921, Saul Zaentz became a media leader in the Bay Area. In the 1950s and 1960s, he worked with Fantasy Records, a major jazz label. In the late 1960s, the company signed Creedence Clearwater Revival, which merged folk roots and rock. In the 1970s, Zaentz became a movie producer. His credits include *One Flew over the Cuckoo's Nest*, *The English Patient*, and *Amadeus*. As a result of his innovative films, Zaentz became a leading independent voice in the industry. The Zaentz Media Center in Berkeley, which he founded, continues to support innovative work in the arts. (Courtesy of the Saul Zaentz Company.)

In the early 1990s, after three generations in their old building, Berkeley Hillel and Lehrhaus Judaica moved into a new home on Bancroft Way across from the University of California campus. The building, pictured above, includes offices, meeting rooms, classrooms, a lounge, and other important facilities. (Author photograph.)

Following Seymour Fromer, Rabbi Stuart Kelman led the East Bay Federation's education programs during the 1980s and 1990s. Among his most successful projects was the advancement of teen education. *Midrasha* programs were established in Berkeley, Oakland, and Contra Costa County, working with high school students in both traditional and creative settings to reinforce their Jewish heritage and increase their investment in doing *mitzvot* (good deeds). In the 1990s, Rabbi Kelman became the spiritual leader of Congregation Netivot Shalom in Berkeley, which he served until 2006. Vicky Kelman, his wife, has been a Jewish educator for many years. She has been a leader in the field of Jewish family education and has spoken and taught widely. In the 1990s and 2000s, she was on the staff of the Bureau of Jewish Education and created a number of innovative and wide-ranging programs for families of all types. (Courtesy of Rabbi Stuart and Vicky Kelman.)

For more than 30 years, Ethelyn Simon was an active member of Oakland's Jewish community. She and her husband, Lawrence (Bud), were members of both Temple Sinai and Temple Beth Abraham and attended services regularly. Ethelyn was also a dedicated Hebrew teacher who tutored dozens of adults every year both in classes and in private sessions. In the early 1980s, she set up a publishing company called EKS to perpetuate her teaching methods and to spread her love of the language. In 2008, EKS's children's book on the bedtime Sh'ma won the prestigious Sydney Taylor Book Award as the best Jewish children's book of the year. (Courtesy of Dena Belzer.)

In 1992, three women—from left to right, Sherry Brown-Ryther, Naomi Tucker, and Rebecca Schwartz—created Shalom Bayit to meet the need for services to assist Jewish women suffering from domestic violence. Over the next decade, it became one of the leading national organizations focusing on this issue. At its 15th anniversary celebration in 2007, Shalom Bayit included dozens of local rabbis, school groups, and a number of foundations among its many supporters. Its efforts have made the issue of violence against Jewish women more prominent than ever before. (Courtesy of Shalom Bayit.)

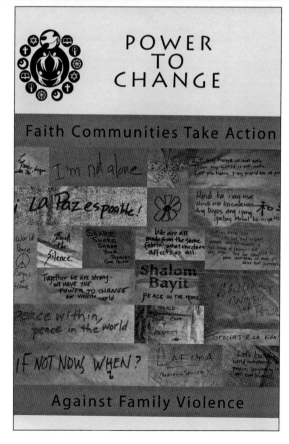

During an interfaith symposium on domestic violence in 1998, Shalom Bayit's staff brought out a sheet of fabric. The attendees participated by writing messages of blessing and peace for those who suffer from domestic violence. Over the years, it has become a symbol of Shalom Bayit's commitment to hope. It has even been used as a chuppah at weddings for the organization's clients. (Courtesy of Shalom Bayit.)

The first Jewish women's organization in America, the National Conference of Jewish Women, was founded in 1894. Oakland's Temple Sinai formed its sisterhood a few years later. Throughout its long history, women have played a leading role in the synagogue's success. In 1994, celebrating a century of Jewish women's activism, 13 former presidents of Temple Sinai Sisterhood gathered for this portrait. (Courtesy of Temple Sinai.)

In 1998, Temple Sinai hired its first assistant rabbi. Over the next decade, Andrea Berlin committed herself to supporting the existing goals of the synagogue and adding her own touches. These included a deep belief in the value of prayer as it can relate to everyday life. Rabbi Berlin's colleagues, Rabbi Suzanne Singer and Rabbi Jacqueline Mates-Muchin, have each added their personal warmth and commitment to Jewish learning and values. (Courtesy of Temple Sinai.)

In the early 1990s, Avram Davis began teaching classes in Jewish meditation techniques. Several years later, the community became formalized as Chochmat HaLev ("knowledge of the heart"). The synagogue is based on merging Eastern and Jewish spiritual traditions; joy and movement are integral to its services. Fifteen years later, the congregation continues to draw interested seekers at its building on Prince Street in South Berkeley. (Author photograph.)

When Robert Alter arrived at the University of California in 1968, very few classes in modern Hebrew literature were being taught in America. Over the next 40 years, the field grew dramatically, in large part as a result of his efforts. Professor Alter has taught and written about the literary qualities of the Bible, culminating in his own translation of the Torah. In addition to teaching and writing, he worked to create the Jewish Studies program at the Graduate Theological Union and was part of the group that formed Tehiyah Day School. (Courtesy of Prof. Robert Alter.)

Henry and Matilde Albers were stalwarts of the Jewish community for many years. Their sponsorship of numerous projects throughout the East Bay has improved the quality of life immensely. After Henry Albers's death, Matilde continued to support a wide array of programs and activities. In 1983, she served as honorary president of the East Bay Federation. As part of its renewal program, the new chapel at Temple Sinai was named in their honor. (Courtesy of the Jewish Federation of the Greater East Bay.)

Jacques Reutlinger immigrated to the United States as a young man. He made and lost two fortunes during his business career and became deeply committed to the welfare of the Bay Area Jewish community. He and his wife, Esther, were generous supporters of the Jewish Federation and its various agencies for many years. When the Home for Jewish Parents moved from Oakland to Danville in 1999, it was named the Reutlinger Center in their honor. (Courtesy of the Judah L. Magnes Museum/Western Jewish History Center, WJHC 1995-006-003.)

In the 1940s, the Jewish Federation established the Home for Jewish Parents in Oakland. It was one of the major projects under the auspices of Lionel Wachs, a leader of the federation and Temple Sinai. By the 1990s, however, the building was in need of significant upgrading. With a major gift from Jacques Reutlinger, a new facility was developed in Danville in Contra Costa County. The Reutlinger Center for Jewish Living opened in 1999. (Author photograph.)

Marcia Falk is a poet, artist, and lecturer. She has translated the Song of Songs from Hebrew and the poetry of Zelda from Yiddish. In 1996, she published the *Book of Blessings*, a re-creation of Hebrew and English prayers from a contemporary, gender-inclusive perspective. The prayer book has been adopted for regular use by a wide variety of communities across the country. In 2008, she was developing *Mizrachs*, a work that combines her prayers and paintings. (Courtesy of Marcia Falk.)

During her time in Oakland, Nancy Katz (left) established herself as an innovative Jewish artist. Her specialty was silk screen prints on fabric and in the creation of personalized *tallit* and other religious objects. Here she works with two clients. (Courtesy of Riva Gambert, Jewish Community Federation of the Greater East Bay.)

Bay Area Midrasha

Every year our young
adults go into the world
with a
Strong Jewish Identity

Thanks to You!

2005-2006
5766

Among the most successful accomplishments in the East Bay community in the 1990s and after was the creation of successful midrasha programs for teenagers. Located in Berkeley, Oakland, Fremont, and in Contra Costa County, they developed a continuum for teens. The Bay Area Midrasha program is divided into two stages: from 8th to 10th grade, ending with confirmation, and high school programs. Alongside the Jewish Community High School in San Francisco, these weekly sessions strengthen the students' Jewish connection through a multitude of classes. This is the brochure of the 2005–2006 Bay Area Midrasha, which operates from Temple Sinai and serves members of all four Oakland synagogues. (Courtesy of Elaine Bachrach.)

The photograph above shows the Oakland Midrasha bulletin board. Midrasha provides teens and their families a wide range of opportunities both to learn and to serve the community. One long-standing project was the preparation of lunch for 120 people at an Oakland homeless center. The weekly program includes arts, academics, and travel. Midrasha also sent teens to Panim al Panim, a national weeklong youth symposium in Washington, D.C. The photograph below shows the 1998 graduating class. Director Elaine Bachrach is standing in the second row at the left. Next to her is Jessica Oleon, who later studied at Hebrew Union College and became a Reform rabbi. (Both courtesy of Elaine Bachrach and Bay Area Midrasha.)

Rene Molho and his wife, Tillie, arrived in Oakland after World War II. Both of them had grown up in Greece and survived the Holocaust. They became members of Temple Sinai and supported the synagogue for many years. One of the passions of their lives was Holocaust education, especially for young people. As part of their legacy, the Molhos created a fund to sponsor Oakland's Holocaust memorial service. Every year, the program draws several hundred people, including the students in the Oakland Midrasha program. (Courtesy of Riva Gambert, Jewish Community Federation of the Greater East Bay.)

Ernie Hollander came to America as a Holocaust survivor. He became a member of Congregation Beth Jacob and was one of its leaders for many years. Like the Molhos, one of his passions was teaching young people about the Shoah and its horrors. He is shown here beside Beth Jacob's Holocaust memorial. (Courtesy of Congregation Beth Jacob.)

In the 1990s and beyond, Beth Abraham was revived by a pair of dedicated rabbis. Mark Diamond (above, center) began the process, and his successor, Mark Bloom (below, holding Torah scroll), continued the revitalization and growth of the synagogue. (Both courtesy of Temple Beth Abraham.)

One of the most important ways to connect people to Judaism is through travel. For many years, the Jewish Community Federation has sponsored missions (trips for leaders to learn about Israel through meetings) and tourist activities. The travelers return with a greater awareness of the state's successes and difficulties and a better understanding of its importance. This photograph was taken during a 1979 mission for adults. The federation also sponsors a four-week summer trip to Israel for teens just after confirmation. The young people return from these experiences with new friends and a unique experience. (Courtesy of the Jewish Community Federation of the Greater East Bay.)

Four

THE WAY WE LIVE NOW
2000–2008

After occupying a portion of 401 Grand Avenue in Oakland for many years, the East Bay Federation moved to this modern building in 2004. The new headquarters at 300 Grand Avenue has office space, meeting rooms, and space for functions hosted by the community. (Author photograph.)

In the late 1970s, Rabbi Alexander Schindler proposed that the Reform movement make a concerted outreach effort to attract non-Jews. Over the following decades, a number of successful programs were developed to inform prospective converts and to educate non-Jews about Jewish ideas. Since 1998, the East Bay's innovative program Building Jewish Bridges has been directed by Dawn Kepler. Her activities have included general Introduction to Judaism classes and targeted efforts directed toward small groups. (Author photograph.)

Paul Hamburg came to the University of California at Berkeley in 1999. Fluent in Hebrew and Yiddish and conversant in several European languages, he has spent a decade building the university's Judaica collections. In addition to deepening the library's holdings in current material, he has worked to acquire several valuable collections from around the world. (Author photograph.)

Among the many novelists in the East Bay, few are as well known as Michael Chabon. *The Amazing Adventures of Kavalier and Clay* (2000), a fictionalized story about the development of superhero comics, won the 2001 Pulitzer Prize for fiction. His next novel, *The Yiddish Policemen's Union* (2007), is an imagined tale about what might have happened if the Jews of Israel had lost the 1948 War of Independence and had been resettled in Juneau, Alaska. It received both the Hugo and Nebula Awards, the two highest honors for science fiction and fantasy fiction. Also published in 2007, *Gentlemen of the Road* recounts the adventures of two medieval travelers and traders. (Courtesy of Michael Chabon.)

The Jewish community has relied on the Grand Bakery in Oakland for its kosher baked goods for over a generation. Its challah is a staple in thousands of homes every Friday evening for Shabbat dinner. (Author photograph.)

For more than a generation, Oakland Kosher Foods on Grand Avenue has been a purveyor of kosher meats and packaged goods as well as foods from Israel. A fire in the fall of 2008 damaged the store, but it was quickly remodeled and reopened in November of that year. (Author photograph.)

While many restaurants in the Bay Area include vegetarian dishes on their menus, there have never been many fully kosher places to eat. The Holy Land Restaurant on College Avenue in Berkeley, which specializes in Israeli fare, is one of them. (Author photograph.)

119

In September 2005, after several years of planning, Berkeley's Congregation Beth El moved into a new facility several blocks from its first home. The plot, formerly the site of a Chinese church, includes a brook that has been planted with native species. The building is shaped in a curve with three points. (Author photograph.)

The sanctuary of the new Beth El includes elegant paneling moved from the original building. The stained-glass window that was above the door on Vine Street was reinstalled at the side of the new sanctuary, and the old metal front doors are attached to the wall outside. One of the most energy-efficient buildings in the region, its heating system draws geothermal energy from several wells under the property. (Author photograph.)

Also in 2005, after extensive renovation and rebuilding, Congregation Beth Israel reopened its building on Bancroft Street in Berkeley. The front of the building repeated the shape of the original entry but in an inviting adobe color. Inside, the new building's library and meeting room was light and airy, with a warm feeling. (Author photographs.)

Sinai Memorial Chapel has been the Bay Area's primary Jewish funeral home since 1905. In the 1990s, Sinai Memorial established a branch in downtown Lafayette, near Temple Isaiah. Susan Lefelstein was its first director. She was one of the first Jewish women funeral directors in the state. As director, she also educated the community and taught numerous people how to perform the rituals surrounding Jewish burials. (Courtesy of Susan Lefelstein.)

The community also began discussing the need for a new Jewish cemetery in the East Bay in the 1990s. With assistance from San Francisco's Sinai Memorial Chapel, six East Bay synagogues developed Gan Shalom Cemetery, which opened in 2008. Located north of Orinda, the new facility will have space for Jewish burials for many years to come. (Author photograph.)

In October 2008, Temple Sinai broke ground for an expanded facility. Because the project required the demolition of its school and office wing, the synagogue moved its daily activities to the campus of Merritt College in the Oakland Hills. The "Sinai Village" included nine portable buildings that would serve as preschool and religious school, offices, and multipurpose room for the interim. During the construction period, the historic sanctuary and social hall remained in use for weekly Sabbath services and meetings. (Author photograph.)

After the ground-breaking, work proceeded quickly. This photograph shows the side of Temple Sinai's historic sanctuary and the rubble from its old education facility in January 2009. (Author photograph.)

In 2008, Temple Beth Abraham also expanded its facility, constructing an annex and acquiring a parking area. The extension includes a new elevator named in honor of Joseph Zatkin. The symbol on the exterior is the Hebrew letter shin, representing one of the names of God. (Author photograph.)

One indication of the success of a synagogue is the commitment of its longtime members. This photograph was taken after a morning minyan at Beth Abraham in February 2009. The group includes several past presidents of the congregation. (Courtesy of Temple Beth Abraham.)

Temple Isaiah has developed as a "home-style" synagogue throughout its 55 years. Members are encouraged to take part in its many activities. Above is a photograph of the interior of the sanctuary today. Below is a recent photograph of the clergy. From left to right are Cantor Leigh Korn, Rabbi Judy Shanks, Rabbi Alissa Forrest, and Rabbi Roberto Graetz. (Both courtesy of Temple Isaiah: below, photograph by Michael Fox.)

As the Jewish community of Contra Costa County grew, there was a need for a day school. In 2001, with assistance from local and national foundations and the East Bay Federation, the Contra County Jewish Day School opened, beginning with kindergarten through third grade. By 2008, the school had a full complement of students through eighth grade. The Judaic program was rigorous but did not focus on a particular movement's positions. For several years, the school used Temple Isaiah's religious school building, but over time, there was a need for a permanent home. With assistance from community members, the school broke ground for its own campus next to Temple Isaiah in 2008. The new complex, scheduled to open in the fall of 2009, will hold over 150 students in its state-of-the-art classrooms. The facility will also include a gym, library/media center, and other services. (Both courtesy of Contra Costa Jewish Day School.)

The East Bay's rabbinic community has a long history of working together across movement lines. The four synagogues in Oakland (Temple Sinai, Beth Abraham, Beth Jacob, and Kehillah) have joined for Tashlich at Rosh Hashanah for several years and have organized an annual evening of learning called Morasha. They also commemorate the Holocaust together. Berkeley and Oakland rabbis and congregants also learn together every year at Shavuot sessions held in the Berkeley JCC. These interactions, and many others, have strengthened the synagogues and the community over many years. The East Bay Board of Rabbis reflects this sense of shared commitment. This photograph, taken at the board of rabbis meeting at Beth Jacob in December 2008, shows 20 clergy, including Renewal, Reform, Conservative, and Orthodox rabbis from Oakland, Berkeley, and Contra Costa County. (Author photograph.)

ACROSS AMERICA, PEOPLE ARE DISCOVERING SOMETHING WONDERFUL. THEIR HERITAGE.

Arcadia Publishing is the leading local history publisher in the United States. With more than 5,000 titles in print and hundreds of new titles released every year, Arcadia has extensive specialized experience chronicling the history of communities and celebrating America's hidden stories, bringing to life the people, places, and events from the past. To discover the history of other communities across the nation, please visit:

www.arcadiapublishing.com

Customized search tools allow you to find regional history books about the town where you grew up, the cities where your friends and family live, the town where your parents met, or even that retirement spot you've been dreaming about.